Lunch Hour

A Play in One Act

John Mortimer

A Samuel French Acting Edition

FOUNDED 1830

SAMUELFRENCH-LONDON.CO.UK
SAMUELFRENCH.COM

Copyright © 1960 by John Mortimer (Productions) Ltd
All Rights Reserved

LUNCH HOUR is fully protected under the copyright laws of the British Commonwealth, including Canada, the United States of America, and all other countries of the Copyright Union. All rights, including professional and amateur stage productions, recitation, lecturing, public reading, motion picture, radio broadcasting, television and the rights of translation into foreign languages are strictly reserved.

ISBN 978-0-573-02149-7

www.samuelfrench-london.co.uk

www.samuelfrench.com

FOR AMATEUR PRODUCTION ENQUIRIES

UNITED KINGDOM AND WORLD EXCLUDING NORTH AMERICA

plays@SamuelFrench-London.co.uk

020 7255 4302/01

Each title is subject to availability from Samuel French,

depending upon country of performance.

CAUTION: Professional and amateur producers are hereby warned that *LUNCH HOUR* is subject to a licensing fee. Publication of this play does not imply availability for performance. Both amateurs and professionals considering a production are strongly advised to apply to the appropriate agent before starting rehearsals, advertising, or booking a theatre. A licensing fee must be paid whether the title is presented for charity or gain and whether or not admission is charged.

The professional rights in this play are controlled by United Agents LLP, 12-26 Lexington Street, London, W1F OLE.

No one shall make any changes in this title for the purpose of production. No part of this book may be reproduced, stored in a retrieval system, or transmitted in any form, by any means, now known or yet to be invented, including mechanical, electronic, photocopying, recording, videotaping, or otherwise, without the prior written permission of the publisher. No one shall upload this title, or part of this title, to any social media websites.

The right of John Mortimer to be identified as author of this work has been asserted by him in accordance with Section 77 of the Copyright, Designs and Patents Act 1988

LUNCH HOUR

First produced at The Playhouse, Salisbury, on the 20th June 1960. Later produced at the Arts Theatre Club, London, on the 18th January 1961, and subsequently transferred to the Criterion Theatre, with the following cast of characters:

(in the order of their appearance)

THE MAN	*Emlyn Williams*
THE GIRL	*Wendy Craig*
THE MANAGERESS	*Alison Leggatt*

Directed by DONALD MCWHINNIE

Setting designed by BRIAN CURRAH

The action of the Play passes in a bedroom in a small hotel near King's Cross

Time—the Present

LUNCH HOUR

SCENE—*A small hotel room near King's Cross. 1 p.m. exactly of a winter's day.*

There is a double bed C, *set diagonally with the foot pointing down* R. *The door is* R *of the bed in the back wall, and there is a window* R *looking out over railway signals and the tops of houses.* L *of the bed is a shilling-in-the-slot gas-fire with a mantelpiece. On the mantelpiece are a Bible, an A.B.C. train time-table and a chiming clock. A wooden chair stands down* L *of the fire.*

When the CURTAIN *rises, the room is empty and the gas-fire unlit. There is a sound of trains off. The clock chimes one. The* GIRL *enters and looks cautiously round the room. She is 23, a textile designer. She wears an overcoat. The* MAN *follows her. He is in his early forties, and is Policy Director of a department in the firm for which the girl works. He wears an overcoat, a hat and horn-rimmed spectacles. The* GIRL *crosses to the fireplace and picks up the A.B.C. She begins to laugh gently. The* MAN *puts his spectacles in his pocket and takes off his hat.*

MAN. Why're you laughing?
GIRL. I don't know. (*She puts the A.B.C. back on the mantelpiece*)
MAN. You're happy?
GIRL. I laugh when I'm hungry too.
MAN (*disappointed*) If you'd rather eat . . .
GIRL. Not at all.

(*The* MAN *throws his hat on the bed. They meet* C)

(*She takes his hands*) You look so big in that overcoat—like a house.
MAN. I'll take it off. (*He unbuttons the overcoat*)
GIRL. Not yet. (*She crosses to the window*) What's this place?
MAN (*crossing to the fireplace*) Just a hotel . . .
GIRL. A hotel?

MAN. By the station. It's convenient . . .
GIRL (*turning*) What for?
MAN. The North of England.
GIRL (*dreamily*) You say the most ridiculous things . . .

(*They meet* C *and hug*)

And no-one knows we're here?

(*They come out of the hug*)

MAN. I'm having a long business lunch with the textile buyers in the Tudor room . . .
GIRL. And I'm alone with an open continental sandwich in a dark corner of the coffee-bar with the rubber plants brushing my cheek.
MAN. And I'm saying: "Well, gentlemen, have a large plate of smoked salmon on the Commissioners of Inland Revenue."
GIRL. But if they looked for us in those places . . .
MAN. They wouldn't find us.
GIRL. No, we're nowhere . . .
MAN. We're here.
GIRL. We've disappeared . . . We don't exist.
MAN. For an hour—or longer. (*He tries to kiss her*)

(*The* GIRL *steps back a pace*)

GIRL. No.
MAN. Business lunches go on for ever.
GIRL (*moving away* R) You can't spend much time on an open continental sandwich.

(*There is a pause*)

MAN (*taking a step back*) You look so small in that overcoat.
GIRL. What do I look like?
MAN. A child in the park on a snowy morning. A woman who's disguised herself to run away to sea . . .
GIRL. Go on talking . . .
MAN. The inexperienced wife of an arctic explorer . . .
(*He pauses*)
GIRL. Go on.

MAN. I've run out.
GIRL. What of?
MAN. Words.

(*The* GIRL *laughs. The* MAN *looks at his watch. The* GIRL *sees this and her laugh dies. There is a pause*)

GIRL. As a matter of fact they're quite good, those sandwiches.
MAN. Are they?
GIRL. And they have other things, too—hamburgers, hot franks in soft floury rolls, great tubes of mustard . . .
MAN. You don't say.
GIRL. Such up-to-date and convenient foods.
MAN. Would you rather be in a coffee-bar?
GIRL. This is much more . . .
MAN. What?
GIRL. Exciting.
MAN. You mean that? (*He steps forward*)
GIRL (*stepping back*) Because I love you.
MAN. And me!
GIRL. How long?
MAN. Since the day you walked into my office . . .
GIRL. With the new design for bedspreads.
MAN. Spanish ivy!
GIRL. You remember!
MAN. And said, "Is this the way to the duplicating department?"
GIRL. And you said . . .
MAN }
GIRL } (*together*) "No, but I'll show you . . ."
GIRL. And you rose up with the light from the window behind you so you appeared all silver——
MAN. Did I?
GIRL. —like a shining statue . . .
MAN. And I took you to Mr Jevons . . .
GIRL. Down the long dark corridors, past the rude and elderly stares of the typing pool . . .
MAN. In the lift.
GIRL. You didn't say a word!
MAN. We certainly established sympathy . . .

GIRL. Oh, love, how it attacks you!

(*The* MAN *steps forward. The* GIRL *steps back*)

You being so quiet in the lift was what I appreciated. Not saying any vulgar remark such as "Where have you been all my life?", or "Is there another one at home like you?" Not even looking . . .

MAN. I was genuinely impressed!

GIRL. Yes.

MAN (*moving to the bed*) And you seemed so lost and uncertain. Like I sometimes feel in that great organization.

GIRL. Such words—from the head of the textile buying department!

MAN. You mean the policy director. (*Thinking of his work*) I'm only the Number Two in that slow-moving set-up. Blast Harris! (*He sits on the bed*)

GIRL (*moving up to his* R) You don't think I'm the sort of girl who comes to a place like this?

MAN (*giving her all his attention again*) No!

GIRL. Then why'm I here?

MAN. My fault.

GIRL (*shaking her head thoughtfully*) I'm the sort to come here.

(*The sounds of a train come through the window*)

What's that?

MAN. The station.

(*There is a pause*)

GIRL (*struck by a thought*) And what about you? Is this how all your lunch hours are spent with some girl or other, and you have to creep out of the office at four o'clock every day for an enormous high tea?

MAN. I've never been here before.

GIRL. Honestly?

MAN. Yes.

GIRL. I'm sorry.

MAN. I love you.

GIRL. Say it again.

MAN. I love you.

GIRL. Mmm. (*She kneels* R *of him*)
MAN. For six months . . .
GIRL. All through the summer.
MAN. With nowhere to go.
GIRL. In spite of the office and your—home life.
MAN. It kept us alive.
GIRL. When we had only a few moments; standing by the tea trolley in the corridor . . .
MAN. Holding hands in the lift . . .
GIRL. You waiting for me in the Embankment Gardens, always first out of the office being on the executive planning side . . .
MAN. Always the same bench.
GIRL. With the flowers standing straight as soldiers and the one-stringed fiddle playing in front of the Tube and tramps asleep under their sheets of newspaper. We had ten minutes a day, now we've got . . .

(*The clock chimes a quarter. They rise. The* MAN *moves away* L)

MAN. Three-quarters of an hour.
GIRL. In this room . . .
MAN. You don't like it?
GIRL (*brushing dust from her knees*) It's not all that sordid really . . .
MAN. We could make ourself more at home—take off our coats. (*He opens his coat*)
GIRL. It's cold.
MAN. I'll light the gas. (*He moves to the fireplace, strikes a match and tries to light the fire*) It needs a shilling. (*He searches his pockets unsuccessfully for a shilling*) Damn!
GIRL. I'll look. (*She burrows in her handbag*) Only sixpences. Would it take two sixpences? (*She goes to the fire,* L *of the man, and puts in her sixpences. But the fire still fails to work*)
MAN. Now you've lost your money.
GIRL. It really doesn't matter.
MAN. Let me give it back to you.
GIRL. It couldn't matter less.
MAN. By the end of the week you'll be short of a coffee.

GIRL. No, really.
MAN. Here. (*Counting money to give her*) Sixpence—sevenpence—ninepence . . .

(*There is a quick knock at the door. The* MANAGERESS *enters*)

GIRL (*as the Manageress enters; almost shouting*) I don't want your money!
MANAGERESS (*coming to the foot of the bed*) Do you want something?
MAN. Ah, yes, a shilling for the gas.
MANAGERESS (*to the Girl, moving a little towards her*) You're cold. A journey does make you cold. Much snow up there?
GIRL. Up where?
MANAGERESS. The North of England.

(*There is a slight pause*)

MAN (*hastily*) Just a powdering of snow, didn't you say, dear?
GIRL (*bewildered*) I've no idea . . .
MAN. The train was going too fast to take a good look.
MANAGERESS. An express?
MAN. That's it.
MANAGERESS. They *can* be fast. Was it the Scotsman?
GIRL. Was what?
MANAGERESS. The Flying Scotsman. (*She moves closer*) My little boy collects engine numbers. Many a time he's seen the Scotsman, waiting at the end of the platform. Puffing and blowing. Would you like a cup of tea?
MAN. Not at all.
MANAGERESS (*to the Girl*) Wouldn't you?
GIRL. Well . . .
MANAGERESS. Isn't that husbands for you? Never appreciate the plain and simple fact that what we wives need after a long cold train journey is a home-made cup of tea. Much snow, did you say?
MAN. She had lunch on the train . . .
MANAGERESS. That doesn't take the place, dear, does it?
GIRL. What of?

MANAGERESS (*moving towards the door*) A cup of tea.
GIRL. Just a ...
MAN. Very short cup.

(*The* MANAGERESS *exits*)

GIRL (*turning to the Man for an explanation, lost and puzzled*) Where've I come from?
MAN. Scarborough.
GIRL (*moving to him*) Why?
MAN. I told her that's where you live.
GIRL. Why should I live in Scarborough?
MAN. Because you're married to me. (*He moves away to* RC)
GIRL (*following him; accusingly*) Then why don't you live in Scarborough, too? What's the matter with you? Can't you stand the climate? You delicate or something?
MAN. I've got digs in London.
GIRL. Thank you very much!
MAN (*patiently*) It's the housing shortage, you see. I've simply got to be near the office. So you're living with your mother in the North.
GIRL (*moving down stage*) Charming!
MAN. Naturally it's a long journey and you don't get up to London very often ...

(*There is a knock at the door.*
The MANAGERESS *enters with a cup of tea. The* GIRL *crosses to the Manageress. The* MAN *moves to the fireplace*)

MANAGERESS. Now drink that down and you'll feel the benefit. You must be worn out.
MAN. She's not very tired ...
MANAGERESS. But they *are* a strain. On a long journey ...
GIRL. What are?

(*The* MAN *picks up the A.B.C. from the mantelpiece*)

MANAGERESS. Running up and down the corridors. Poking their noses into the first class. Playing with the chickens in the guard's van and locking themselves in the toilets.

(*The* MAN *puts the A.B.C. back on the mantelpiece*)

GIRL (*lost and confused*) It's like a sort of dream.
MANAGERESS. Never seen London before? This is their first glimpse of the smoke?
GIRL. What's she saying?
MANAGERESS. Their first Tube and double-decker? If I know anything that'll mean the Chamber of Horrors for you this afternoon. (*She sits on the bed*)
GIRL. Is she out of her mind?
MANAGERESS. You know what mine does on a long journey?
GIRL. How can I possibly tell?
MAN. Well, I think you've finished your tea.
GIRL. It's hot.
MAN. You don't want it?
GIRL. Might as well...
MANAGERESS. On a long journey mine always takes out his box of crayons and chalks the marks of an infectious disease on his face before the journey commences.
GIRL. What for?
MANAGERESS. To ensure privacy in the compartment.
GIRL (*interested*) Does it work?
MANAGERESS. Nine times out of ten. And if not...
GIRL. What?
MANAGERESS. He can make it pretty sticky for those that do venture in.

(*The* MAN *tries to speak*)

But why I mentioned the Chamber of Horrors was this. When his cousins come on a visit from the North, it's always downstairs at the Tussaud's they make their first port of call.
MAN. Ours doesn't like that sort of thing. (*He moves towards the Girl*) Finished your tea, dear?
MANAGERESS. They don't like the Tussaud's? (*She rises and moves back a little*)
MAN. Gentle, nervous kiddies, weak on history... (*He takes the cup from the Girl and crosses to the Manageress*) You'll want to wash the cup up.

GIRL (*following him*) Who are we talking about now?
MAN. Our children.
GIRL (*breathless*) How many?
MANAGERESS (*accusingly*) Three.

(*The* MAN *takes a quick drink of tea*)

GIRL. Three?
MANAGERESS. Two boys and then your husband got his girl.
GIRL. Congratulations!
MAN. The time's getting on.
MANAGERESS (*taking the cup and saucer*) I've got things to do, too. They'll be excited though, seeing auntie after all this time . . .

(THE MANAGERESS *exits*)

GIRL. Who's auntie?

(*The* MAN *tries to kiss her, but she turns her face away. She repeats insistently*)

Who's auntie?
MAN (*moving down* L) My married sister. She lives near the heath.
GIRL. Is that a good thing?
MAN. It's a godsend, as I told the Manageress. She can look after the kiddies.
GIRL. They're with her now . . .
MAN. She's quite capable—a trained nurse, that's what she used to be.
GIRL (*moving away down stage*) Well, I should think they must be totally confused in their small minds.
MAN. Confused?
GIRL. Bewildered.
MAN. But why . . .
GIRL. For heaven's sake! What's it all about? Those quiet, gentle, little children with no sense of history are woken out of their warm beds at what must have been a cruelly early hour in Scarborough and dragged all the way to London only to be dumped with some ex-matron of an aunt while we scurry off to a small private hotel in King's Cross!

(*The* MAN *tries to speak*)
And another thing about those children—where are they going to spend the night?
   MAN (*guiltily*) I thought . . .
   GIRL (*challengingly*) Well?

   (*There is no reply*)
(*Incredulously*) You can't mean . . .
   MAN. You'll all want to get back.
   GIRL. To *Scarborough?*
   MAN. Well, it is home. Only temporary, of course.

   (*The* GIRL *rushes to the mantelpiece and seizing the A.B.C. turns the pages with bitter determination. The* MAN *moves* C *to the foot of the bed*)

   GIRL. Scarborough. Saxmundham. Scably . . . Scarborough! Pop. forty-three thousand, nine hundred and eighty-five. Early closing Wed. London two hundred and three miles! Four hundred and six miles a day you would laughingly see me travel with three young children who can't be all that grown up and responsible, bearing in mind the fact, which you very well know, that I am not a day over twenty-three.
   MAN (*moving down* R; *miserably*) The boys were twins.
   GIRL. You know what.
   MAN. What?
   GIRL. *I don't think you're fit to have children!* I can't think why you went on breeding for the selfish reason of wanting a girl after the twins, and, when I've given birth to them and all that, you can only think of sending them on pointless and exhausting train journeys practically the whole length of the British Isles . . .
   MAN (*moving towards her to* LC) Listen!
   GIRL (*moving down to him*) They'll be dropping asleep by the time we get home, and suppose we can't find a taxi . . .
   MAN. Please, let me explain . . .
   GIRL. Four lives you've got in your hands.
   MAN. I was desperate!
   GIRL. *Then why couldn't you come up to Scarborough for the week-end?*

(*The clock chimes the half hour*)

MAN. There's so little time . . .
GIRL (*moving away down* L) Such inconsiderate behaviour!
MAN (*following her a little way*) Do we have to talk?
GIRL. I certainly think you owe me an explanation.
MAN. I'm in love with you.
GIRL. You have odd ways of showing it. If that's the way you treat all your wives!
MAN (*moving towards her*) You're not my wife!
GIRL. That's one consolation.
MAN. We love each other!
GIRL. What about it?
MAN. Let's be thankful. Let's celebrate the revolution. Our victory against the dull rulers of our lives! Look at this room! Look, what we've achieved!
GIRL. What?

(*They look round at the room*)

MAN. A beach-head in a dark grey enemy country! A small clearing in the jungle behind our own impermanent and wobbling stockade. A place on our own! Does it matter what I had to say to win it for us? (*He moves* C)
GIRL. Sometimes it matters.
MAN (*turning to her*) What?
GIRL. What you have to say.
MAN (*moving to the foot of the bed*) It doesn't matter.
GIRL. Anyway I'm curious to know.
MAN. What?
GIRL. How you got us here.
MAN. Later on . . .
GIRL. No, now! (*She moves up stage*) I want to know exactly who I am. I puzzle myself at the moment.

(*The* MAN *takes a quick look at his watch, and then sits on the bed*)

MAN. Well, I was walking along the street and I happened to catch sight of this hotel. It seemed small and . . .
GIRL. Unostentatious?

MAN. So I was faced with a problem. How could a man and a . . .
GIRL. Woman?
MAN. Exactly. Without any kind of luggage . . .
GIRL. We've got no luggage!
MAN. Take a room for an hour, in the middle of the day . . .
GIRL. Your only time for adventure.
MAN. That was the problem. I solved it!
GIRL (*moving towards him*) You did?
MAN. After a little thought. I said we wanted somewhere to talk . . .
GIRL (*after a slight pause*) To what?
MAN. To talk.
GIRL (*after another slight pause*) It's incredible . . .
MAN. The Manageress understood.
GIRL. She hadn't got to face the endless journey back with three uncontrollable children.

(*The* MAN *rises and moves* RC. *The* GIRL *follows*)

Anyway, we could have done that in the lounge.
MAN. What?
GIRL. Talked.
MAN. No privacy.
GIRL. Or at our married sister's—the one who lives up by the heath.
MAN (*after a moment's hesitation*) Well, no—we went into that. It wasn't at all a practicable idea.
GIRL. Why not?
MAN (*turning down stage*) Well, there's no point in digging up that old buried hatchet.
GIRL. What?
MAN (*turning to her*) You see, you've never got on with my married sister.
GIRL. Never?
MAN. She stayed away from the wedding.
GIRL (*moving down* LC) Oh, did she?
MAN. Since then there's been a bit of an east wind between us.
GIRL. I should think so.

MAN. Just one of those little failures of understanding that happen in all families. It wasn't at all your fault. You certainly did your best, I told the Manageress that, but, well there it is.

GIRL. What a lot you told that Manageress!

MAN (*moving towards her*) To get the room.

GIRL. Yes.

MAN. All for that.

GIRL. I suppose so.

MAN (*moving to her*) Because I honestly loved you. (*He tries to kiss her*)

GIRL (*breaking away from him down* RC) What's she got against me?

MAN. Who?

GIRL. Aunty.

MAN. Nothing.

GIRL. What kept her away from the wedding then?

MAN. Well, you know how people are, old-fashioned ideas.

GIRL (*turning to face him*) You mean you *told* her?

MAN. What?

GIRL (*pointing at the bed*) About this afternoon.

MAN. Now where have you got me? (*He looks at her in confusion and then moves away to the fireplace*)

GIRL. Where've you got yourself? Do you ever stop to ask yourself that? I mean, whose side are you on, anyway?

MAN. Yours, of course.

GIRL. Well, it doesn't look so very much like it! Keeping up such friendly relations with a woman who wouldn't even condescend to turn up at the reception my father can ill afford, leaving our children to the tender mercy of this starched and creaking old matron with her grey moustache and celluloid cuffs, who treats me (*crying*) like a nasty mess in the out-patients. (*She moves* C) I should have thought you might show a little more honesty and integrity and act more like the bright shining husband in glittering armour that you let me think you were when you tricked me . . .

MAN. I tricked you?

GIRL. You let me believe I was the only thing that mattered in your life.

MAN. You are!
GIRL. Now it seems any old aunt gets more consideration . . .
MAN. *It's not true!*

(*There is a pause. Then she moves over to him, and they break down in each other's arms*)

GIRL (*sobbing*) I'm sorry.
MAN. I'm sorry, too.
GIRL. You are?
MAN. I'm sorry we had to have all these—complications.
GIRL. I didn't mean you tricked me.
MAN. I know you didn't.
GIRL. I just thought you might write to her, that's all.

(*The* MAN *takes a step back*)

Nothing abusive, of course, nothing to bring us down to her level. Just "in view of your attitude, it would no doubt be more convenient if you let at least twenty years elapse before paying your first call". You never wrote her a line like that?
MAN. Of course I didn't. Because . . .
GIRL. You never came out in the open in support of me?
MAN. Because . . .
GIRL (*advancing on him, her anger returning*) And who is she, anyway? Trained nurse? What's that? Florence Nightingale? Madam Curie? What's her great achievement? Rolling up some royalty in a blanket bath?

(*The* MAN *sits in the chair down* L *of the fireplace*)

Being present at the removal of a so-called appendix from a so-called film star in a nameless nursing home in Hammersmith? I know those trained nurses! Heartless! (*She moves away* C) Knit and gossip all night and drink cocoa in the face of death! (*She comes back to him*) Just let her try and hold down my job which isn't just automatic and calls for some creative imagination! We do two hundred versions of

the Spanish ivy pattern now—and not one of them a repeat.
MAN. I know.
GIRL. Well, you should appreciate that.
MAN. Don't worry about her.
GIRL. Why not?
MAN. She's not real.
GIRL. She's real to me! (*She moves to the side of the bed*)

(*The* MAN *follows her*)

(*She turns*) Snobs! That's one thing we don't tolerate in our family, thank God. That's one type of person that just seems to me so low that I couldn't get any lower if I got down on my stomach and wriggled under that door! My father's been an ordinary printer for the best part of thirty years, but there's only one type of person that he wouldn't give house-room to in any circumstances and that's a *snob*. Also he can't put up with the Irish. But he's never been the sort to go poking and prying into someone's past history and drawing aside his skirts and refusing to attend the ceremony of marriage and turning young children against their mother when her back is turned.

MAN. Look at me. (*He sits her on the bed and himself sits beside her*)
GIRL. Well?
MAN. We're alone.
GIRL. Yes?
MAN. Remember. Nothing else exists. Everyone else in the world has faded away. All our friends and families—

(*The* GIRL *tries to interrupt*)

—and relations. We're alone here together. Fixed and solitary in this moment of time. No-one can come near us. (*He moves close, about to kiss her*)

(*There is a quick knock at the door. The* MANAGERESS *enters*)

MANAGERESS. I've found a shilling for you! (*She goes to the gas-fire and puts in the shilling*) Now. Who's got a match?

(*The* MAN *and the* GIRL *rise. The* GIRL *moves down* R. *The* MAN *moves to* R *of the fireplace and silently hands the Manageress a box of matches*)

Of course you'll hardly be needing all that shilling's worth now, will you? (*There is a pause*) You'll be good Samaritans to the next occupants. (*She lights the gas*) There now! That makes it more cosy and home-like, doesn't it? (*There is a pause*) I always say, after a nice coal fire I like a nice gas-fire.

(*There is another pause. The* MAN *holds out his hand for his matches. The* MANAGERESS *puts them in her pocket*)

A nice fire is nice to talk by, and you'll want to get on with your discussion.
MAN. Yes.
MANAGERESS. If you give me that change then.
MAN. We had two sixpences.
GIRL (*after searching her bag*) We put them down the slot.
MAN. I've only got ninepence after the taxi.
MANAGERESS (*stonily*) Well, you asked me to get the shilling. I distinctly heard you.
MAN. Yes, we did.
MANAGERESS. Naturally I assumed you had change to give me for it.
MAN (*taking out his wallet*) I've got a pound. (*He takes out a pound note*)
MANAGERESS. That's hardly very convenient. How can I change a pound at short notice?
MAN. I don't know.
MANAGERESS. I had to *send out* for the shilling!
GIRL. We've given you a shilling already.
MANAGERESS. What?
GIRL. My two sixpences straight down the slot with no result at all!
MANAGERESS. Really . . .
GIRL. You can't expect to get any more out of us.
MANAGERESS. Me? I'm not making a penny! That goes straight to the North Thames Gas Board.

GIRL. With the price of the room add on two shillings for gas . . .
MANAGERESS. I've never had any complaints before.
GIRL. How much was the room?
MAN. Well . . .
GIRL. Tell me, how much?
MAN (*turning up stage*) Two guineas.
GIRL. For an hour!
MANAGERESS. It's no concern of mine if you have to leave after an hour.
GIRL. Two guineas an hour! Forty-eight guineas a day——

(*The* MAN *looks at the Manageress*)

—for a broken-down old bed and peeling wallpaper and a gas-fire that's daylight robbery and the use of a chiming clock and the A.B.C. of trains! We're in the wrong business! (*She moves* C *towards the Manageress*) I knew it didn't pay to be creative!

(*The* MANAGERESS *moves* C *to meet the Girl. The* MAN *tries to part them during the following speech, and failing, moves up* R *to the window*)

MANAGERESS. I've had twenty-five years in the King's Cross area as Manageress of this private hotel and I've never heard words like that spoken to me before.
GIRL. Well, it's about time you did. And what about that little boy of yours?
MANAGERESS. What about him!
GIRL. Playing round the station. Going round all the telephones and pressing the button B's, I should think most likely.

(*The clock chimes three-quarters of an hour*)

MANAGERESS. I've a very good mind . . .
GIRL. I'm perfectly sure there's some law . . .
MANAGERESS. I put myself out to get you a little warmth . . .
GIRL. Some people work for their living!
MANAGERESS. Because you've had a long day!

MAN (*coming down to the Manageress in despair and forcing the pound note on her*) Take this.

(*The* MANAGERESS *takes the note and crosses to the door. The* MAN *moves to the side of the bed. The* GIRL *crosses* L)
Don't come back with the change.

MANAGERESS. Peeling wallpaper! I tell you, I've had government officials sleep in this very room. Indian gentlemen. And very nicely spoken. Only I was sorry for the fix you and your husband was in I agreed to take you for the hour. He wanted to talk to you, you see. On a serious matter! *Well he might!*

(*The* MANAGERESS *exits. There is a pause. The* MAN *crosses to the door*)

MAN. I thought we'd never get rid of her. (*He locks the door*)

GIRL (*after a pause*) Well, she's gone now.

(*The* MAN *returns to* C. *Another pause*)

MAN. We've only got fifteen minutes left...
GIRL. Now it's coming.
MAN. Darling, won't you take your coat off?
GIRL. I dread it.
MAN (*moving to her*) No, come on...
GIRL. I'm sorry. (*She goes to him and takes his hands*) I know it's silly and stupid and weak of me perhaps. But ever since I was a child, quite a young girl, you understand, this has been something I have dreaded and I knew it was coming the moment I stepped into this room. I know that was why you brought me here. But whatever the good reason you may very well have had, I don't want it to happen.
MAN. But we discussed...
GIRL (*stepping back from him*) It's just a horrible feeling I get in the pit of my stomach. I've felt it coming on and perhaps that was why I was a bit sharp with that old girl, although heaven knows when you have to count every penny, and sometimes travel on the Tube with nothing but

a hopeful wink at the ticket collector, it makes you sick to see money demanded on that exhorbitant scale! However. If anyone says to me, "Could I have a word with you?" it's always and quite certainly the one word I don't want to hear.

MAN. What do you mean?

GIRL. The head designer may say: "I'd like a word with you in the office," or my father says: "We'd like to talk to you if you can arrange to be home early next Wednesday," or they say: "This Underground ticket looks a bit exhausted, could we talk to you about it?"and whatever it is they have to say I don't want them to say it, so please forgive me if all I can think of at this moment is *I don't want you to talk to me*.

(*There is a pause*)

MAN. I'm not going to talk.

GIRL (*after a pause*) What do you mean?

MAN. You've got nothing to worry about.

GIRL. Why did she say that then?

MAN. Say what?

GIRL. That you wanted me—for a serious talk?

MAN. Please listen. (*He takes her hands and tries to get her to sit on the bed*)

GIRL. No!

MAN (*sitting on the bed himself*) We've got so little time, and if this goes wrong . . .

GIRL. What?

MAN. What've we got left?

GIRL. It seems I've always got the children . . .

MAN (*pulling her gently down to sit on his L*) Don't you see, you're the one oasis in the desert of my days and nights. The one person that's saved me from suddenly growing old and spent among the business lunches, and the Scandinavian lamp-shades, and the bright red hang-it-yourself wallpaper. So if we've got a few minutes, don't let's waste them.

GIRL (*after a pause*) No. (*She pauses again*) I did love you. When you stood up so silver against the light—and when I got out of the lift and a draught of air from the print-room blew up my skirt I saw you turn away your eyes and spare me the look of curiosity—and I thought—here's someone quite exceptional in this building riddled with intrigue and romance . . .

(*They kiss. The* MAN *tries to take her into his arms*)

What were you going to say?
MAN. When?
GIRL. I mean it must have been something of great importance.
MAN. It was nothing.
GIRL. To bring a person all that way on the train to hear it.
MAN. Nothing.

(*The* GIRL *rises and stands back from him, looking at him carefully, as if for the first time*)

GIRL. I mean you're not the sort of man that wants a woman to travel all that way just to discuss the weather, are you! It must have been something serious and terrible you had to disclose.
MAN. I never thought . . .
GIRL. And that journey! What about it? Hour after hour, watching the frozen lines, trying to keep the children quiet. All the time the thought going round in my head—he's got something to tell you. What's it going to be? What's so bad it can't be stuck in an envelope or said out over the telephone? Are you the sort of man that would keep a woman in suspense like that?
MAN. Of course I'm not.
GIRL. But it must be days ago you asked me to come up. How do you think I've been feeling since then. *Do you think I've had much sleep? Do you care?*
MAN. Don't you understand?
GIRL. No. You haven't told me yet. (*She faces out front*) Let's face it now. Let's get it out of the way at last!
MAN. There's nothing to say.

(*There is a pause. Then they look at each other*)

GIRL. Or are you the sort of man that would bring his wife all this way to tell her something of great importance which might affect their whole lives and then shut up as tight as an oyster the moment he was in her presence!

MAN. No.

(*There is a pause. The* GIRL *rises and crosses to his* R)

GIRL. Coming to look at you clearly with the light in front of you I think that's the sort of man you might be.

MAN. I'm not. Listen . . .

GIRL. Because it can only be one thing, can't it? For me to have come all this way to hear it, it can only be one logical thing.

MAN (*interested in spite of himself*) What?

GIRL. That it's over. Finished. (*She sits on the foot of the bed*) You don't care about the children and me any more. Oh, it was very convenient for you, having me tucked away at the end of a long cold railway line! It gave you plenty of scope to cultivate your friendships in the office. To take girls down in the lift and lure them into strange hotels during the lunch hour. You were able to take full advantage of the two hundred and three miles you so carefully put between us. So now you'll write a letter starting "No doubt this will come as a terrible shock to you . . ." which you want me to hand in to give you your so-called freedom. Isn't that what it all comes to, if you had the courage to put it into words?

MAN. I never thought of that!

GIRL. Yes, you did. When you started to talk to the Manageress! When you told her the story. The story had to end, didn't it? Can you think of a different ending?

MAN (*after thought*) There must be one, somewhere.

(*The clock begins to chime two o'clock. The* GIRL *rises first— then the* MAN *rises*)

GIRL. It's over. (*She looks at him with tenderness and pity*) You should never have explained our presence.

(*The* GIRL *exits*)

MAN. Wait. Wait a minute.

But the GIRL *has gone. The* MAN *looks round the empty*

room. *He puts on his hat and stoops to the gas-fire. He hesitates, puts on his spectacles, and then turns off the gas. He crosses to the downstage corner of the bed, and there notices that his overcoat is undone—the overcoat that he never took off. He turns towards the door, braces himself to face the world outside, and exits as—*

the Curtain *falls*

FURNITURE AND PROPERTY PLOT

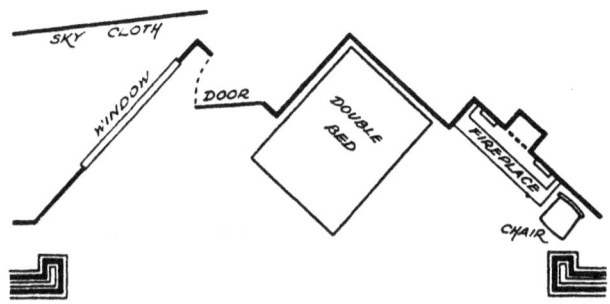

On stage: Bed. *On it:* bedding
Mantelpiece. *On it:* Bible, (up stage) Clock (c) A.B.C. train time-table (down stage)
Net curtains on window
Wooden chair (down L)
Rug on floor beside bed
Gas meter. *On it:* padlock
Window closed
Window curtains open
Door closed
Fire off
Gas meter knob in correct position with slot open

Off stage: Cup of tea
1/- piece

Personal: MAN: Wrist-watch, matches, 3d. piece, 6d. in coppers, wallet with £1 note
GIRL: Handbag with purse containing two 6d. pieces

LIGHTING PLOT

Property fittings required: a gas-fire, the meter type (practical)
Interior. The same scene throughout
THE MAIN ACTING AREAS are at the door R, by the bed C and LC

To open: Effect of daylight from the window R

Cue 1 MANAGERESS: ". . . next occupants." (**Page** 16)
She lights the gas
Bring in gas-fire

Cue 2 The MAN puts on his spectacles and turns off
the gas (**Page** 22)
Cut out gas-fire

EFFECTS PLOT

Cue 1	At the rise of the CURTAIN *Sound of trains*	(Page 1)
Cue 2	At the rise of the CURTAIN *Clock chimes one*	(Page 1)
Cue 3	GIRL: ". . . sort to come here." *Sound of trains shunting*	(Page 4)
Cue 4	GIRL: ". . . now we've got . . ." *Clock chimes the quarter*	(Page 5)
Cue 5	MAN: ". . . sevenpence—ninepence . . ." *Quick knock at the door*	(Page 6)
Cue 6	MAN: ". . . London very often . . ." *Knock at the door*	(Page 7)
Cue 7	GIRL: ". . . the week-end?" *Clock chimes the half hour*	(Page 10)
Cue 8	The MAN and GIRL are about to kiss *Quick knock at the door*	(Page 15)
Cue 9	GIRL: ". . . think most likely." *Clock chimes three quarters*	(Page 17)
Cue 10	MAN: ". . . be one, somewhere." *Clock chimes two*	(Page 21)

MADE AND PRINTED IN GREAT BRITAIN BY
LATIMER TREND & COMPANY LTD PLYMOUTH

MADE IN ENGLAND

www.ingramcontent.com/pod-product-compliance
Lightning Source LLC
Chambersburg PA
CBHW070455050426
42450CB00012B/3288